ABOVE: *This engraving first appeared in the 'Sporting Magazine' in 1793 and is the only authentic picture of cricket on the first Lord's Ground.*

FRONT COVER: *A cricket match at Rugby School in 1889, after H. Jamyn Brooks.*

CRICKETING BYGONES

Stephen Green

Shire Publications Ltd

CONTENTS

Set in 9 on 9 point Times roman and printed in Great Britain by City Print (Milton Keynes) Ltd, 16 Denbigh Hall Industrial Estate, Bletchley, Milton Keynes.

For my brother Dudley

ACKNOWLEDGEMENTS

My grateful thanks are due to Mr John Arlott and Mr Christopher Martin-Jenkins for allowing me to use and adapt material on *Vanity Fair* cartoons which originally appeared in various issues of the *Cricketer* back in 1953. Mr Gordon Ross and Mr Alan Pryer helped in various ways whilst I owe more than I can say to the scholarly work of Miss Diana Rait Kerr. My secretary, Mrs Fay Ashmore, has struggled valiantly with my writing and turned my incomprehensible scribbles into a faultless typescript. My colleague, Mr Michael Lucy, was very helpful in making preparations for the photographers to take the illustrations which adorn these pages. To all who have helped I am truly thankful. All the photographs are of items in the MCC collection at Lord's.

This Doulton stoneware three-handled loving cup, depicting W. G. Grace in action, was made in 1880.

CRICKET.

A GRAND MATCH WILL BE PLAYED

In LORD's NEW Cricket Ground,

St. JOHN's WOOD MARY-LE-BONE,

On THURSDAY JUNE the 6th. 1816, and the following day, between TWO SELECT ELEVENS of all ENGLAND.

For Five Hundred Guineas a Side.

The WICKETS to be Pitched at ELEVEN o'Clock.

PLAYERS,

Lord F. Beauclerk	Lord Clifton
Lord Sunderland	Hon. D. Kinnaird
F. Ladbroke Esq.	Sir T. Jones
B. Aislabie Esq.	G. Osbaldeston Esq.
T. Woodbridge Esq.	E. H. Budd Esq.
W. Ward Esq.	J. Poulett Esq.
J. Tanner Esq.	— Lewis Esq.
A. Schabner Esq.	T. Lloyd Esq.
T. Wills Esq.	W. Barton Esq.
T. Brown Esq.	T. Lord Jun. Esq.
B. Dark.	N Mann.

ADMITTANCE SIX PENCE, Good STABLING on the GROUND.

The Cricket Laws, BATS, BALLS, and STUMPS to be had at the Ground or at Mr. LORD's HOUSE in Upper Glofter Street,— the nearest Carriage way is up the New Road oppofite Mary-le-bone Work-houfe. NO DOGS ADMITTED.

Craft, Printer, Well's-Street, Oxford-Street.

The match bill for a fixture at Lord's in 1816. Many of the famous players of the time are listed as taking part. Large sums of money were at stake in such matches.

HISTORICAL INTRODUCTION

The origins of cricket are ancient and un-recorded. This has not, however, prevented endless speculation as to the most likely way in which the game could have evolved. The most plausible explanation is that cricket is derived from the word *cric*, which is the old English for a shepherd's crook. This is the word used in the earliest English rendering of the twenty-third psalm, where the Authorised Version reads 'Thy staff'. Certainly the earliest illustrations of a cricket bat show an implement which looks remarkably similar to the crics or crooks carried by the Bethlehem shepherds at the Nativity of our Lord, as depicted in medieval wall-paintings such as the one in Cocking church, near Chichester.

According to this theory, the wicket would have been the wicket gate into the sheep fold. One can imagine shepherd boys out in the fields trying to relieve their boredom by hitting a pine cone with their crick or crook whilst at the same time defending the wicket gate into the fold.

The earliest undoubted reference to cricket is contained in a document, dated 1598, in the borough archives of Guildford. This refers to cricket being played in the town at the grammar school about fifty years previously – i.e. about 1550 or just before the beginning of the reign of Elizabeth I.

During the seventeenth century there are about fifty references to cricket in all. With the exception of 'stray' references to the game in Dublin (1656) and in Aleppo (1672), these invariably relate to places in the south-east of England. Many cricketers incurred the wrath of the Puritans by indulging in the game on the Lord's Day and so we can roughly plot the spread of the game by noting the places where the local players appeared in court! Later in the century the game seems to have begun to appeal to the aristocracy. This may have been because, during Cromwell's Commonwealth, the Royalist gentry had to withdraw from public life. Whilst they were isolated on their country estates they had to find time-consuming occupations to satisfy their energy and cricket with its long drawn-out procedures was an obvious attraction.

It was in the eighteenth century that the game spread to the majority of the English counties as well as to some other parts of the world. For instance, the troops which were sent to quell the Forty-five rebellion are popularly supposed to have been instrumental in bringing the game to Scotland. Two significant developments of the latter half of the eighteenth century were the rise to fame of the Hambledon Club in Hampshire and the founding by Thomas Lord in 1787 of the cricket ground in Marylebone which bears his name.

The Marylebone Cricket Club soon took over where Hambledon had left off and Lord's Ground quickly became the centre of the game. MCC assumed responsibility for the laws of the game and in 1805 there was commenced the first match between Eton and a Harrow eleven, which included among its players Lord Byron. This series between the two schools is the oldest to have survived in the Lord's fixture list.

During the first half of the nineteenth century there was much controversy as to whether it was lawful for a bowler to abandon the traditional underarm methods and to adopt a round-arm and later an overarm delivery. The formation of the All England Eleven in 1846 by William Clarke of Nottingham produced the first truly representative national side. One of the players was Nicholas Wanostrocht, who usually adopted the pseudonym of 'Felix'. He was a gifted amateur artist and many of his sketches of the All England Eleven players and of their matches have survived.

Overseas cricket tours soon became established, commencing with visits to North America in 1859 and to Australia in 1861-2. The arrangement for these tours was often very haphazard until MCC took over responsibility for them in 1903. The sponsors, for example, of the first tour of Australia were a catering firm, Messrs Spiers and Pond. They really wanted Charles Dickens to undertake an antipodean lecture tour under their auspices and the cricket arrangements were made very much as a second best!

The first Australian team to visit England was the aboriginal side which toured in 1868. Nine years later the Melbourne Cricket Club staged the first Test Match ever played, whilst in 1880 – again much as an afterthought right at the end of the season – the first international match to be played in England took place at the Kennington Oval. Two years later on that ground England lost to Australia for the first time in a Test Match played on home soil. The *Sporting Times* published a mock obituary notice lamenting the death of English cricket. This ended with the words 'The body will be cremated and the ashes taken to Australia'. The following winter of 1882-3, the Hon Ivo Bligh took out a team to Australia. After one of the matches some Australian ladies collected the ashes of a bail and placed them in an urn, which they presented to the England captain. One of the ladies was to marry Ivo Bligh and it was she who, after her husband's death, presented the Ashes urn and other accompanying items to Lord's. Nowadays the Ashes only metaphorically travel to Australia when that country wins the series – the actual urn rests in the

This picture by Sablet of Mr Hope of Amsterdam playing cricket in Italy with his friends (1792) is one of the finest of cricket paintings.

Cricket Memorial Gallery at Lord's.

Towards the end of the nineteenth century cricket teams were touring all parts of Queen Victoria's far-flung empire. The latter days of the Victorian era and the reign of Edward VII were a golden age of English cricket with the majestic Dr W. G. Grace as its dominant character. Dr Grace was probably the most famous person in England after the Queen herself and possibly Mr Gladstone and mementoes of him can be found in all shapes and sizes. He figures on stevengraphs, postage stamps, plates and statuettes, whilst there are many paintings and engravings in which his massive form can be seen. Many other great cricketers adorned the game and only the advent of the First World War in 1914 brought the golden age to a close. Perhaps symbolically, W. G. Grace died in 1915 and with him were to perish in the following three years far too many young cricketers of promise.

It did not take the game long, however, to recover and the inter-war years were also to witness much fine cricket. During this time New Zealand, India and the West Indies were admitted to Test cricket. Above all this period saw the phenomenal rise to fame of Don Bradman. By the end of the 1930s England was able to fight back with the aid of such great players as Hutton and Compton, who followed in the tradition of Hobbs and Woolley.

The Second World War caused the interruption – and in a large number of cases the finish – of many careers of promise but the golden summer of 1947 showed that the game had lost none of its seductive appeal. The major worry of cricket administrators began to lie in the realm of finance but the reintroduction of commercial sponsorship brought a new vitality to the game, as well as a more dynamic image. The County Championship continues to be the backbone of the first class game, however, whilst the demand for tickets for Test matches and the vast number of telephone calls to discover the latest score prove that cricket still holds a unique place in the affection and interest of an enormous number of English men and women.

Cricket is mainly played in the countries of the British Commonwealth but there is also a devoted following in such places as Denmark, Holland and parts of the United States. In spite of some inevitable tensions and stresses as the game of necessity has become more commercially orientated, it has acted as a unifying force in a fragmented world and it has brought much pleasure to innumerable people.

Few games have such an artistic and literary heritage. One of the ways in which people have for long enjoyed the game –

particularly during those seemingly endless winter evenings – has been by the collecting of 'cricketana'. This book seeks to indicate some of the main types of cricketing items which are collected by devotees of the game.

The large curved shape of an eighteenth-century bat is shown beside a twentieth-century example signed by members of the MCC team in Australia, 1932-3 – the famous 'Bodyline Series'.

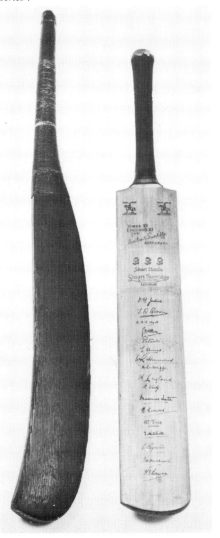

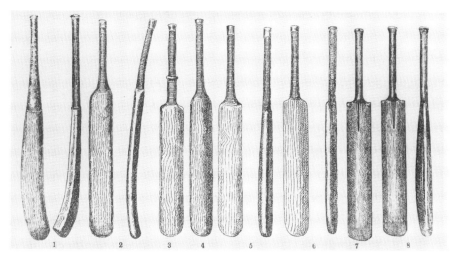

The evolution of the cricket bat: 1, 1743; 2, 1771, weight 5 pounds (2268g); 3, 1790 – a double-handed bat which belonged to a man with a crippled hand, who wore an iron strapped to his wrist; 4, 1792; 5, 1800, weight 2¾ pounds (1247g); 6, 1827, weight 2¾ pounds (1247g); 7, 8, modern bats, weight 2 pounds 5½ ounces (1063g), showing the splicing.

CRICKET BATS

The modern bat consists of a willow blade with a cane handle layered with thin strips of rubber, bound with twine. Over this is stretched a rubber sheath. The cane extends from the shoulders into the heart of the willow and this projection is known as the splice. The maximum dimensions are 4¼ inches (108 mm) in width and 38 inches (965 mm) in length. The average bat weighs around 2 pounds 5 ounces (1049 g) but there has never been a weight limit. In the nineteenth century our ancestors often used a 4 pound (1814 g) bat.

The evolution of the bat is perhaps best studied with the aid of the accompanying illustration. The earliest surviving bat is housed in the pavilion at Kennington Oval. It is dated 1729 and it is inscribed 'J.C.' for John Chitty. Probably the most comprehensive collection showing the evolution of the bat can be seen in the Memorial Gallery at Lord's Cricket Ground. The early bats were enormous and heavy. They must have stung the batsmen very much when they made a vigorous hit. The earliest spliced bats in the MCC collection date from the middle 1830s whilst the first sprung ones appear in the 1860s.

The fullest account of the development of the cricket bat is contained in Hugh Barty-King's remarkable and original work entitled *Quilt Winders and Pod Shavers*. The book contains a particularly valuable list of virtually all the known major manufacturers of cricket bats and balls – names like Clapshaw, Duke, Cobbett, Dark, Warsop, Bussey, Gunn and Moore, Wisden, Surridge, Gradidge, Gray-Nicolls, Odd and Duncan Fearnley, to list but a few.

People tend to collect cricket bats for one of two reasons: either the bat in question was used in some historic match, or else it has been inscribed with the autographs of leading players. It is usually easier to come by the latter category. For the serious would-be collector in this field, as indeed in most other branches of cricketana, the best move is probably to write for the catalogues issued by Messrs Phillips (7 Blenheim Street, London W1) for their specialist sales. This firm has for some time made a speciality in the sale of cricketing bygones and they hold auctions at regular intervals.

A bowler who took three wickets with consecutive deliveries was sometimes presented with a top hat. This was the origin of the expression 'a hat-trick'. Later an ornamental 'hat' was sometimes given instead. This example dates from 1900, and the plaque on the ball commemorates the same feat.

CRICKET BALLS, STUMPS AND BAILS

Contrasted with the bat, the cricket ball has changed little over the years. It is made of hand-stitched leather dyed red whilst the interior consists of cork wound with twine. It must weigh between 5½ and 5¾ ounces (156-163 g) – a ruling which has been in force since 1774. Previously a ball had to weigh between 5 and 6 ounces (142-170 g), as laid down in the 1744 code. The circumference has to be not less than between 8 13/16 inches and 9 inches (224-229 mm). In 1838 the circumference had to be between 9 and 9¼ inches (229-235 mm) but this was altered in 1927 to the present regulation.

One of the earliest references to a cricket ball is contained in William Goldwin's Latin poem *In Certamen Pilae,* written in 1706. The earliest cricket ball in the Lord's collection is the one off which William Ward made his historic 278 when playing for MCC against Norfolk in 1820. This was to remain a record score for an innings at Lord's until it was bettered 105 years later in 1925.

Cricket balls do not tend to survive in such quantities as bats. Sometimes, how-ever, a particularly noteworthy feat will be commemorated by the addition of an en-graved silver band recording the bowler's performance. The best known names in cricket ball manufacture include Duke, Dark, Wisden, Ives, Martin, Reader, Bussey, Ayres, Gradidge, Gray-Nicolls, Surridge and Lillywhite Frowd.

One of the most notable achievements a bowler can accomplish is to take the hat-trick. This feat was so called because in days gone by a top hat was presented to a bowler who took three wickets with con-secutive deliveries. One such example has survived at the seat of Lord Saye and Sele, Broughton Castle near Banbury. Later in the nineteenth century an ornament in the shape of a top hat came to be presented instead. A good example can be seen in the famous Long Room at Lord's Cricket Ground.

Few stumps and bails have survived. The earliest stumps in the MCC collection, however, are believed to date from 1798. In days gone by players and spectators used to grab a stump or a bail after an important match and keep it as a souvenir.

CRICKETING COSTUME

A concise summary of the development of cricket dress can be found on pages 158-60 of *Wisden Cricketers' Almanack*, 1966. It is very rare indeed to come across any items of cricket dress dating from before 1850. MCC does possess, however, in the Lord's collection a virtually complete cricketing outfit which was worn by Henry Daw of Christchurch about 1820. The authorities at the Victoria and Albert Museum say that this, as far as they know, is the only sporting outfit for any game to have survived in England from that period.

It is possible to find attractive items of cricketing dress from after 1850 although these are still rare until one reaches the opening years of the twentieth century. In the 1870s cricketers often wore 'pillbox' caps which were similar to those worn by page-boys. Colourful belts were also worn at this time – these were frequently adorned with attractive buckles depicting cricketing scenes. These are quite often found in people's gardens. One suspects that when the belts became faded or tatty they were then used for rough wear and subsequently lost after an energetic spell of digging! Old pads are rare although MCC has one which was used by E. G. Wenman about 1850. The Lord's collection also has a pair of lightweight 'skeleton' pads, which were popular with players such as Victor Trumper in the opening years of the twentieth century. Batting gloves also rarely survive – the oldest in the Lord's collection was used by G. L. Jessop in the Test matches of 1902.

This is a typical belt buckle with a cricket theme. Motifs of this kind were very popular in the mid Victorian period.

9

ABOVE: *W. G. Grace's colourful belt, with several typical Victorian buckles depicting cricket scenes.*

LEFT: *The MCC touring blazer worn by Sir John Masterman (later Vice-Chancellor of Oxford University) on the visit to Canada in 1937.*

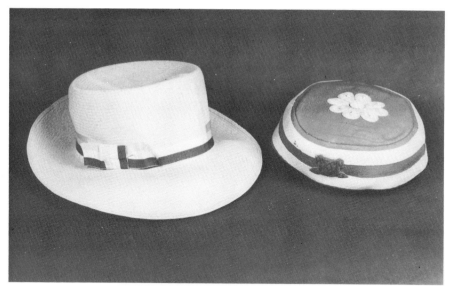

ABOVE: *A Panama hat (left) used by lady cricketers of the White Heather Cricket Club in 1922, and an MCC 'pillbox' cap (right) dating from about 1880.*

RIGHT: *An I Zingari blazer formerly the property of Mr G. O. Allen. I Zingari is the oldest of the wandering cricket clubs, having been founded in 1845.*

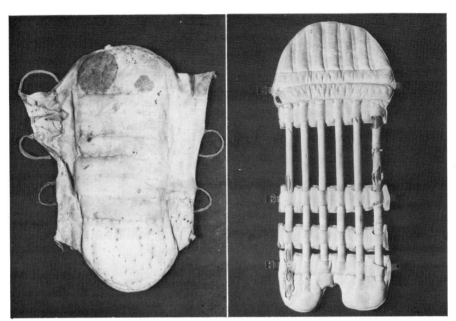

ABOVE LEFT: *A buckskin leg pad used by E. G. Wenman, the Kent wicketkeeper, about 1850.*

ABOVE RIGHT: *Skeleton pads were popularised around 1900 by such players as Victor Trumper.*

BELOW: *A batting glove worn by G. L. Jessop in Tests at the beginning of the twentieth century.*

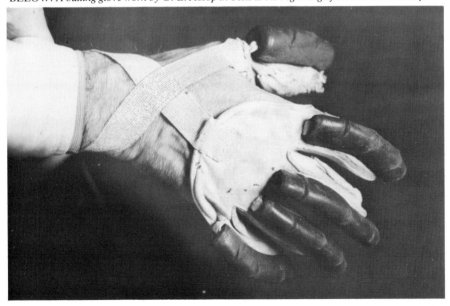

CRICKET BOOKS

Books on cricket are numerous and fortunately there are a number of firms which have specialised in this aspect of collecting. Perhaps the largest stock of new and second-hand books about cricket is held by Mr E. K. Brown of Bevois Mount, Church Street, Liskeard, Cornwall. Mr J. W. McKenzie of 12 Stoneleigh Park Road, Ewell, Epsom, Surrey, specialises in the production of illustrated catalogues and in the reprinting of rare books which were originally published long ago. Other dealers in cricket books include Mr M. J. Wood of 2 St John's Road, Sevenoaks, Kent, and Southern Booksellers of 84 Bohemia Road, St Leonards on Sea, East Sussex.

The literature on the game is immense but there is a very useful survey of the most important books on pages 575-91 of *The Barclays World of Cricket* (edited by E. W. Swanton and published by Collins in 1980). The game has also been well served by E. W. Padwick in his most professional *Bibliography of Cricket* (Library Association for the Cricket Society, 1977).

Financial considerations will influence the collector in deciding what he can obtain but, in addition, most people will have to calculate how much physical space they can devote to this side of their hobby. *Wisden Cricketers' Almanack*, for instance, has been published every year since 1864 and thus a complete set comprises well over a hundred volumes and will cost the would-be purchaser thousands of pounds. Despite this, every serious collector aims to own a complete

set of *Wisden* even if this is becoming an increasingly difficult task to accomplish.

It is not always easy to decide what constitutes a cricket book. For example, a man may have played cricket for his school and university and then gone on to become a diocesan bishop. Does his biography (which may well deal mainly with ecclesiastical matters) deserve a place in a cricket library? Similarly the history of an English village may be written with only a chapter (or less) devoted to the saga of its cricket team. Difficulties in selection abound but therein lies half the interest of the subject.

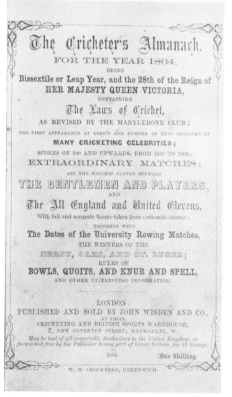

The title page of the first edition of Wisden, the most celebrated of all cricket annuals.

13

AUTOGRAPHS

Cricket lovers have for a long time collected the autographs of their heroes on the field of play. Recently the present writer was shown the autographs of the All England Eleven which must have been collected by an unknown Victorian enthusiast well over a hundred years ago. This is a field where it is important to link up with other enthusiasts and it is also a case where the insertion of a small advertisement in one of the cricketing periodicals or in *Exchange and Mart* can work wonders. Many cricketers, past and present, are very helpful in replying to courteous and reasonable correspondents. The latter should *always* enclose a stamped addressed envelope. Many cricketers have no secretary and in any case this is a common courtesy now that the cost of postage is so high.

Letters written by the significant figures of the game, such as Dr W. G. Grace (who was a prolific if not very informative correspondent), can sometimes be obtained from the main dealers in autographs. The best known is perhaps Winifred A. Myers, 91 St Martin's Lane, London WC2.

PHOTOGRAPHS AND POSTCARDS

A few private individuals have built up impressive collections of historic cricket photographs and postcards. The earliest known photographs of the game were taken in 1857 by no less a person than Roger Fenton. He was celebrated at the time for the vivid photographs which he took in the Crimean War. Fenton's cricket photographs were recently sold by auction at Christie's and other examples of early views of the game can from time to time be found in antique shops.

PAINTINGS

Cricket has been the subject of a very large number of paintings – possibly only the equestrian sports can rival the game in this respect. Many great artists, such as Turner, Hudson, de Wint, Landseer, G. F. Watts and Zoffany, have depicted the game. Cricket paintings frequently appear in the catalogues issued by Christie's, Sotheby's and Phillips. Apart from some Victorian watercolours, the prices fetched are, however, prohibitive for the ordinary collector.

The largest and finest collection of cricket art is to be found at Lord's but examples of the genre can be seen in the art galleries at Carlisle, Derby, Kendal, Leeds, Leicester, Newcastle upon Tyne, Port Sunlight, Sheffield and Wakefield, as well as at the Fitzwilliam Museum at Cambridge and the great national collections at the Tate Gallery, the Victoria and Albert Museum and the British Library. Further examples can be found in the stately homes at Antony, Blenheim, Breamore, Lamport, Petworth, Rockingham and Tissington. There must be many more examples.

However, as John Arlott has pointed out, in most of the best oil paintings the game and the players are only incidental to the main theme. In many of the landscapes the cricketers are relatively insignificant figures who might often just as well be playing another game. Similarly in a large number of the portraits the youthful sitters are depicted holding cricket bats and carrying cricket balls but these are usually little more than props to add human interest to the painting. In modern times, however, Lawrence Toynbee has made a speciality of painting impressionistic action studies of cricketers. In this work he has been greatly aided by the fact that he is an enthusiastic club cricketer. Another prominent artist, John Ward RA, has painted some fine portraits of recent players and cricket administrators. There ought also to be scope for collecting cartoons about the game–for example the work of Tom Webster.

London County Cricket Club.

"St. Andrew's," Lawrie Park Road,

SYDENHAM, *Jul* 22   1900.

ABOVE: *A typical hasty note written by W. G. Grace, who was a conscientious, if not a very exciting, correspondent.*

BELOW: *Roger Fenton's views of the Royal Artillery versus Hunsdonbury match in 1857 are the earliest known cricket photographs.*

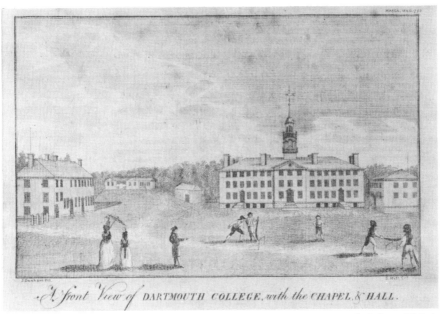

A rare engraving from the Massachusetts Magazine showing cricket at Dartmouth College, USA, in 1793. The first record of American cricket is in 1709.

PRINTS AND ENGRAVINGS

The collecting of prints and engravings connected with the game is perhaps the best way to enjoy cricket art at only a modest cost. The earliest cricket picture is dated 1739 and is after Gravelot. It is entitled 'Youth playing at Cricket' and is delightful. There are some further rare eighteenth-century engravings, of which the best known are 'Cricket in the Artillery Ground, Finsbury' (1743); the print which originally appeared in 1793 in the *Sporting Magazine* entitled 'Grand Cricket Match played in Lord's Ground, Marylebone, on 20th June and following day between the Earls of Winchelsea and Darnley for 1,000 guineas' (the only surviving picture of cricket being played on the original Lord's Ground); and the various prints which accompanied the broadsheets containing the early laws of cricket. Another favourite of the period was 'Miss Wicket and Miss Trigger'. A rare example came from America and originated in the *Massachu-*

setts Magazine in 1793. It is entitled 'A Front View of Dartmouth College, with the Chapel and Hall' and it shows a game of cricket in progress in the foreground.

There are a number of well known cricket aquatints which can be found without too great a difficulty. Two particular favourites are 'Cricket at White Conduit House: 1784' and 'Ireland's Royal Gardens, Brighton'. Other famous cricketing scenes include 'North-east View of Cricket Grounds at Darnall, near Sheffield, Yorkshire' after Robert Cruikshank and Pollard's 'Cricket Match'. Rowlandson's 'Rural Sports' (1811) depicts women cricketers in a far from flattering manner!

The best known of all cricket prints was produced by W. H. Mason of Brighton. It was first published in 1849 and it bears the title 'A Cricket Match between the counties of Sussex and Kent, at Brighton'. Many pirated copies subsequently appeared.

16

An 'Ape' cartoon of the Hon. Alfred Lyttelton (1857-1913). He is the model of a well dressed amateur wicketkeeper in his I Zingari colours.

A 'Spy' cartoon depicting Martin Bladen, seventh Lord Hawke (1860-1938), captain of Yorkshire from 1883 until 1910.

(Alfred Mynn) and 'The Batsman' (Fuller Pilch). There are in addition three major team groups: 'The Two Elevens of the Town and University of Cambridge in 1847', 'The Eleven of England Selected to Contend in the Great Cricket Matches of the North for the Year 1847' and 'The United All England Eleven'. There are also some very attractive lithographs depicting individual players, most notably John Corbet Anderson's 'Sketches at Lord's'.

Cricket prints (and one should not forget that many views of the public schools show a game in progress) can be readily acquired from the specialist dealers. The Parker Gallery of Albemarle Street, London W1, has possibly the biggest stock relating to the game.

A great deal of enjoyment can be obtained from the collecting of *Vanity Fair* cartoons. Since it is not always easy to identify the person depicted from the accompanying caption, a list of the more prominent cricketing personalities who appeared as the subjects of *Vanity Fair* cartoons is given on page 31. These cartoons may be bought in a wide variety of places – a selection can, for instance, usually be found in the concentration of print shops around the Charing Cross Road in London.

According to John Arlott, one of the greatest experts on the subject, the finest period for cricket art was in the middle of the nineteenth century when the technique of lithography had been fully mastered. There are less than a hundred cricket lithographs, of which the finest are those by G. F. Watts entitled 'Play', 'Forward', 'The Draw', 'The Cut', 'Leg Half-Volley', 'Leg Volley', 'The Bowler'

In 1905 a series of forty-eight drawings by A. Chevallier Tayler was published under the title of *The Empire's Cricketers*. The Fine Art Society first produced them individually in weekly parts and later they appeared as a bound edition. Many people like to collect them – their appearance is distinctive since they were printed on dark grey paper.

CIGARETTE CARDS

The collection of cricketing cigarette cards is not to be despised. In his *Picture of Cricket* (1955) John Arlott remarked: 'the finest pictorial record of cricket in this century is presented in cigarette cards.' Quite often the only illustration available nowadays of a player of the days gone by is to be found in this medium. It is estimated that around two thousand players are shown in this way.

The most attractive cricketing cigarette cards were issued between 1896 (when Wills led the way with a charming set) and the start of the Second World War. It is believed, however, that the first ones to depict cricketers were issued in Australia in the 1880s.

Wills issued further sets in 1901, 1908, 1928 and 1929 whilst they had rivals in the Churchman series of 1928 and 1936 and those distributed by Player in 1930, 1934 and 1938.

ABOVE LEFT: *A sketch of Clem Hill by A. Chevallier Tayler from 'The Empire's Cricketers' (1905). Hill captained Australia in 1910-11 and 1911-12 and was one of the greatest left-handed batsmen.*
ABOVE RIGHT: *R. H. Spooner by A. Chevallier Tayler. Reggie Spooner (Lancashire and England) was one of the most elegant amateur batsmen of the golden age before the First World War.*
BELOW: *Three cigarette cards depicting cricketers, from a set issued by Wills in 1896. They are the earliest English cards in the MCC collection.*

ABOVE: *These cigarette cards showing well known players come from sets issued by Wills in 1928 and 1929.*

BELOW: *Cigarette cards depicting (from the left) T. E. Sidwell, the Leicestershire wicketkeeper, and two of the greatest players of the inter-war period, M. W. Tate and W. R. Hammond.*

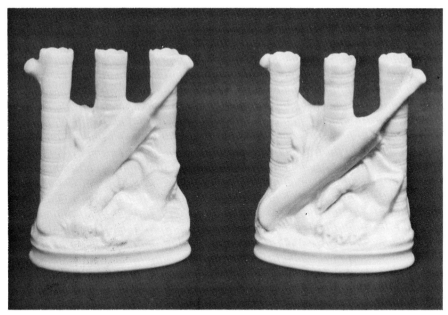

A pair of Belleek ware spill holders made in Ireland about 1880.

CERAMICS

In the field of ceramics there are various items which are well worth collecting, including the two large Staffordshire figures of about 1855 which are believed to represent Julius Caesar and George Parr. Care must be taken to ensure that one is buying genuine antiques and not modern copies although even the latter have some value. There are some rarities in the MCC collection at Lord's. Two of the oldest consist of a Staffordshire soup tureen and meat plate depicting Windsor Castle with a cricket match in the foreground. These are dated *c* 1820. The Memorial Gallery also possesses a very rare set of Staffordshire spill holders of *c* 1841. These depict a batsman (Fuller Pilch), a bowler (William Lillywhite) and a wicketkeeper (Thomas Box).

The various pieces of Doulton ware depicting cricketers which were produced in the last years of the nineteenth century are proving popular with collectors whilst the Coalport dessert plates which were issued to commemorate W. G. Grace's hundredth century in 1895 have long been in demand. Those plates which were used at the celebration dinner at Bristol in January 1896 have the table plan of the diners printed on the back and are very valuable. The plate was subsequently issued on a larger scale but without the table plan.

More recently the Royal Worcester Company has made a small series of bone china plates bearing reproductions of the signatures of the members of the various touring teams. In addition Nubern Products have issued a plate to commemorate the winner of the County Championship each year. Some beautiful souvenirs were produced by the Crown Derby Company in 1970 to commemorate the centenary of the Derbyshire County Cricket Club. Some delightful pieces of Webb Corbett crystal were also made in honour of this event.

21

ABOVE: *A plate produced by the Royal Worcester Company to celebrate England's winning of the Ashes in 1953.*

BELOW: *A plate made to commemorate Colin Cowdrey's hundredth century in 1973. It was inspired by a previous plate in honour of W. G. Grace.*

Mid Victorian Staffordshire figures said to represent Julius Caesar and George Parr.

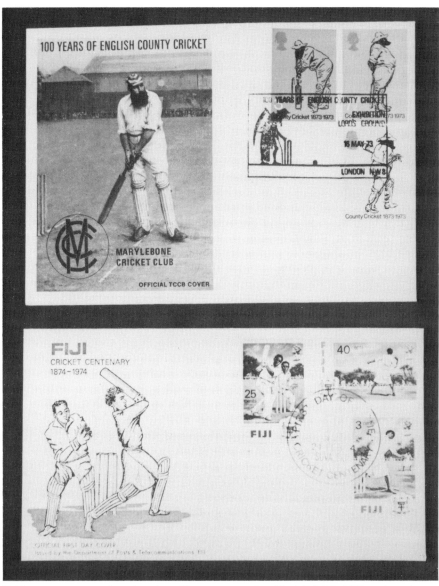

Cricket postage stamps have been issued by many countries. (Top) Britain's 1973 set showed some sketches of W. G. Grace by Harry Furniss of 'Punch' fame. (Bottom) Fiji's cricket centenary, 1974.

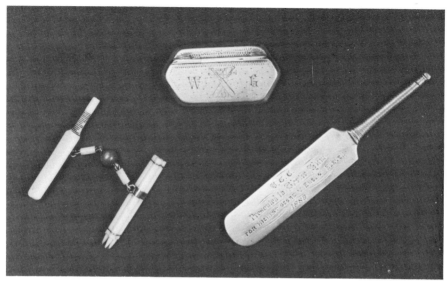

W. G. Grace's snuff box; carved ivory coat links sold by Lillywhite Brothers and Company in 1853; and a miniature cricket bat presented by Ballarat Cricket Club in 1889.

MISCELLANEOUS ITEMS

There are quite a number of silver items which are connected with the game and which bear cricketing motifs. These have usually taken the form of trophies or of special presentations (ranging from epergnes and christening mugs to toast racks) and they naturally command large prices at sales and auctions.

Items of 'cricketana' exist in many forms. These range from gramophone records, tiles, snuff boxes, scorecards and watches to exotic items such as pieces of statuary, horn drinking cups and cut crystal goblets. Stevengraphs are a case in point. These were pictures made by T. Stevens of Coventry and were embroidered in coloured silk. Two of these are connected with cricket – those depicting 'The First Over' and W. G. Grace. Similarly one can obtain a piece of Goss china showing the monument at Hambledon.

Other people have made a thematic collection of cricket postage stamps, of which there have been a large number in recent years, commencing with the Cape Verde issue of 1962. Victorian cricket songs with their attractive covers also make a good field for study whilst other collectors become engrossed in the acquisition of cricket ties. Cricket handkerchiefs have been fetching high prices at recent auctions. The early ones depicting the eighteenth-century versions of the laws of cricket have long been in demand but recently there has been an upsurge of interest in the nineteenth-century handkerchiefs. These depict such subjects as the MCC Jubilee Match in 1837, the Eleven of England 1847, the England team in Australia 1861-2 and W. G. Grace's century of centuries.

Perhaps enough has already been written, however, to prove that the potential collector of cricketana will not be short of suitable material which he may acquire! He can then follow his favourite game in the summer months and keep his interest throughout the off season.

ABOVE: *Emile Roche's christening mug (1852), bearing cricketing motifs, and a Victorian toast rack made up of representations of bats, balls, stumps and bails.*

BELOW: *A set of brass buttons issued by the Islington Albion Club, flanked by members' badges for the Sydney and Perth cricket grounds.*

CRICKET.

A GRAND MATCH!

WILL BE PLAYED AT THE

COPENHAGEN CRICKET GROUND,

Islington,

ON THURSDAY, AUGUST 9, 1849,

BETWEEN ELEVEN GENTLEMEN OF THE

ISLINGTON ALLIANCE CLUB,

AND ELEVEN GENTLEMEN OF THE

WINDSOR & ETON

JUNIOR CLUB,

WICKETS PITCHED AT HALF-PAST TEN O'CLOCK.

N.B. Good Stabling.

A splendid match bill for a game to be played at Islington in 1849.

27

ABOVE: *A handkerchief produced to commemorate the hundredth century by Jack Hobbs.*

BELOW: *A collection of admission cheques. These became less popular when membership cards were introduced. (The famous MCC red pass was introduced in 1880).*

28

2d. Lord's Ground

ENGLAND v. AUSTRALIA.

FRI, SAT, MON, JUNE 27, 28, 30, & TUES, JULY 1, 1930.

ENGLAND		First Innings		Second Innings	
1 Hobbs	Surrey	c Oldfield, b Fairfax	1	b Grimmett	19
2 Woolley	Kent	c Wall, b Fairfax	41	hit wicket, b Grimmett	28
3 Hammond	Gloucestershire	b Grimmett	38	c Fairfax, b Grimmett	32
4 K. S. Duleepsinhji	Sussex	c Bradman, b Grimmett	173	c Oldfield, b Hornibrook	48
5 Hendren	Middlesex	c McCabe, b Fairfax	48	c Richardson, b Grimmett	9
6 A. P. F. Chapman	Kent	c Oldfield, b Wall	11	c Oldfield, b Fairfax	121
7 G. O. Allen	Middlesex	b Fairfax	3	l b w, b Grimmett	57
8 Tate	Sussex	c McCabe, b Wall	54	c Ponsford, b Grimmett	10
9 R. W. V. Robins	Middlesex	c Oldfield, b Hornibrook	5	not out	11
10 J. C. White	Somerset	not out	23	run out	10
11 Duckworth	Lancashire	c Oldfield, b Wall	18	l b w, b Fairfax	0
		B 2, l-b 7, w , n-b 1	10	B 16, l-b 13, w 1, n-b	30
		Total	425	Total	375

FALL OF THE WICKETS

1-13	2-53	3-105	4-209	5-236	6-239	7-337	8-363	9-387	10-425
1-45	2-58	3-129	4-141	5-147	6-272	7-329	8-354	9-372	10-375

ANALYSIS OF BOWLING

Name	1st Innings					2nd Innings				
	O.	M.	R.	W.	Wd.	N-b.	O.	M.	R.	W.	Wd.	N-b
Wall	29.4	2	118	3	..	..	25	2	80	0	1	
Fairfax	31	6	101	4	..	1	12.4	2	37	2		
Grimmett	33	4	105	2	..	..	53	13	167	6		
Hornibrook	26	6	62	1	..	..	22	6	49	1		
McCabe	9	1	29	0	..	..	3	1	11	0		
Bradman							1	0	1	0		

AUSTRALIA		First Innings		Second Innings	
1 W. M. Woodfull	Victoria	st Duckworth, b Robins	155	not out	26
2 W. H. Ponsford	Victoria	c Hammond, b White	81	b Robins	14
3 D. G. Bradman	New South Wales	c Chapman, b White	254	c Chapman, b Tate	1
4 A. F. Kippax	New South Wales	b White	83	c Duckworth, b Robins	3
5 S. J. McCabe	New South Wales	c Woolley, b Hammond	44	not out	25
6 V. Y. Richardson	South Australia	c Hobbs, b Tate	30		
7 A. G. Fairfax	New South Wales	not out	20		
8 W. A. Oldfield	New South Wales	not out	43		
9 C. V. Grimmett	South Australia				
10 T. M. Wall	South Australia	Innings closed.			
11 P. M. Hornibrook	Queensland				
		B 6, l-b 8, w 5, n-b	19	B 1, l-b 2, w , n-b	3
		Total	729	Total	72

FALL OF THE WICKETS

1-162	2-393	3-585	4-583	5-643	6-672	7-	8-	9-	10-
1-16	2-17	3-22	4-	5-	6-	7-	8-	9-	10-

ANALYSIS OF BOWLING

Name	1st Innings					2nd Innings				
	O.	M.	R.	W.	Wd.	N-b.	O.	M.	R.	W.	Wd.	b.
Allen	34	7	115	0	4	..						
Tate	64	16	148	1	..		13	6	21	1		
White	51	7	158	3	..		2	0	8	0		
Robins	42	1	172	1	1	..	9	1	34	2		
Hammond	35	8	82	1	..		4.2	1	6	0		
Woolley	6	0	35	0	..	..						

Umpires —Chester and Oates.   Scorers —Callicott and Ferguson.

The figures on the Scoring Board show the batsmen in.

Play commences 1st day at 11.30. 2nd, 3rd and 4th days at 11.

Luncheon at 1.30 p.m.   †Captain   *Wicket-keeper

Stumps drawn 6.30 each day.

TEA INTERVAL—There will probably be a Tea Interval at 4.30-4.45 but it will depend on the state of the game.

ENGLAND WON THE TOSS.

Scorecard of the Lord's Test, 1930. A magnificent 254 by the youthful Don Bradman for Australia ensured England's defeat by seven wickets, but centuries by Duleepsinhji and Chapman meant that England was not disgraced.

A CORRECT STATEMENT OF THE

GRAND CRICKET MATCH,

Betwixt Sheffield and the County of Leicester,

At Darnall, on Tuesday, September 7th, 1824, for 100 Sovereigns. Qa Side

LEICESTER First Inning.		SHEFFIELD First Inning.	
Earl, bowled by Marsden,	36	William Petty, caught by Allen	12
Shelton, bowled by Dawson,	13	William Barber, caught by Cheslyn	1
Davis, caught by Wright,	14	T. Marsden, run out	2
Gambles, bowled by Dawson,	0	John Wright, caught by Gambles	2
Sharp, caught by Woolhouse,	4	Littlewood, bowled by Colston	5
Allen, bowled by Wright,	6	Woolhouse, bowled by Gambles	0
Cheslyn, Esq. caught by do.	1	Dearman, caught by Pallet,	29
Squires, bowled by Marsden,	2	G. E. Dawson, caught by Shelton	38
Owston, not out	23	E. Vincent, caught by Earl	13
Pallet, bowled by Wright	2	James Youle, stumped by Davis,	4
Colston, caught by Wright,	5	Webster, not out	3
Byes	4	Byes	1
Total	110	Total	110

LEICESTER Second Inning.		SHEFFIELD Second Inning.	
Earl, run out	3	Woolhouse, caught by Gambles,	2
Shelton, bowled by Marsden	8	Barber, bowled by Gambles	9
Sharp, do. by Wright	0	Wright, bowled by Colston	3
Davis, do. by Marsden	14	Marsden, not out	54
Gambles, caught by Woolhouse	21	Dearman, run out	0
Owston, bowled by Marsden	15	Dawson, bowled by Allen	3
Allen, caught by Vincent	11	Youle, bowled by Allen	1
Squires, not out	16	Webster, bowled by Colston	8
Cheslyn, Esq. caught by Dawson	3	Vincent, caught by Gambles,	12
Colston, do. by Wright	8	Petty, caught by Allen	3
Pallet, bowled by Marsden	0	Littlewood, bowled by Gamble	7
Byes	4		
Total	103	Total	102

Slaters, Printers, Fargate, Sheffield.

Scorecard of a match at Darnall near Sheffield in 1824. This ground was probably the most important in the North of England until 1829, when the Hyde Park ground came into prominence.

VANITY FAIR CARTOONS OF
CRICKETING PERSONALITIES

Property: 1st Earl of Dudley.
A man of position: Lord Lyttelton.
The Eccentric Liberal: E. Horsman.
This fell sergeant – strict in his arrest: Lord Charles Russell.
Marshal of the ceremonies: Hon G. W. Spencer Lyttelton.
The Duke of Sport: Duke of Beaufort.
Cricket: W. G. Grace.
Spencer: Sir Spencer Ponsonby-Fane.
Handsome Fred: General Frederick Marshall.
The Demon Bowler: F. R. Spofforth.
Georgie: Lord George Hamilton.
Liverpool: Dr J. C. Ryle.
Kent: Lord Harris.
Isandula: Lord Chelmsford.
Agriculture: 2nd Earl of Leicester.
Australian Cricket: G. J. Bonnor.
English Cricket: Hon A. Lyttelton.
Wiltshire: Rt Hon W. H. Long.
W. W.: W. W. Read.
A man of law and broad acres: Mr Justice Bray.
Fred: 6th Earl of Bessborough.
Oxford Cricket: H. Phillipson.
Monkey: A. N. Hornby.
A Big Hitter: A. E. Stoddart.
Sammy: S. M. J. Woods.
Yorkshire Cricket: Lord Hawke.
Oxford Athletics: C. B. Fry.
Mr Attorney: 1st Earl Loreburn.
I Zingari: J. L. Baldwin.
The Earl of Dartmouth: 6th Earl of Dartmouth.
South Bucks: Viscount Curzon (6th Earl Howe).
Mike: R. A. H. Mitchell.
The Consol Market: C. F. C. Clarke.
Fred: General Frederick Marshall?
Ducker: D. H. McLean.
Ranji: K. S. Ranjitsinhji.

Hampshire: E. G. Wynyard.
Patiala: Maharaja of Patiala.
Haileybury: E. Lyttelton.
The Croucher: G. L. Jessop.
4th Division: Hon N. G. Lyttelton.
The Lobster: D. L. A. Jephson.
Bobby: R. Abel.
A Flannelled Fighter: Hon F. S. Jackson.
Trinity: Reverend H. M. Butler.
Winchester: Reverend H. M. Burge.
Repton, Oxford and Somerset: L. C. H. Palairet.
Yorkshire: G. Hirst.
Plum: P. F. Warner.
Ivo: Lord Darnley – formerly Hon Ivo Bligh.
Cricket, Railways and Agriculture: Viscount Cobham.
An artful bowler: B. J. T. Bosanquet.
In his father's steps: Lord Dalmeny.
Bow Street: R. H. B. Marsham.
The Master of the Blankney: E. Lubbock.
Tom: T. Hayward.
Reggie: R. H. Spooner.
Forty-six centuries in eleven years: J. T. Tyldesley.
Cricketing Christianity: Reverend F. H. Gillingham.
Father: C. M. Wells.
A Century Maker: K. L. Hutchings.
Arthur: Sir A. C. Lucas.
Charlie: C. Blythe.
A tested Centurion: J. B. Hobbs.
The Champion County: E. W. Dillon.
Rhodes the Second: Sir Abe Bailey.
   In addition Thomas Hughes appeared in the issue for 8th June 1872, C. C. Clarke on 19th November 1896, P. M. Thornton on 22nd March 1900 and J. R. Mason was depicted by Spy in a supplement to the *World*.

FURTHER READING

Allen, D. R. *A Song for Cricket*. Pelham Books, 1981.
Altham, H. S. *A History of Cricket*. Allen and Unwin, fourth edition 1948.
Barty-King, H. *Quilt Winders and Pod Shavers*. Macdonald and Jane's, 1979.
Birkett, N. *The Game of Cricket*. Batsford, 1955.
Bowen, R. *Cricket – A History*. Eyre and Spottiswoode, 1970.
Cardus, N. and Arlott, J. *The Noblest Game*. Harrap, 1969.
Colman, J. *The Noble Game of Cricket*. Batsford, 1941.
Laver, J. *The Book of Ties*. Seeley, Service, 1968.
Padwick, E. W. *Bibliography of Cricket*. Library Association for the Cricket Society, 1977.
Peebles, I. A. R. and Rait Kerr, D. M. *Lord's 1946-1970*. Harrap, 1971.
Savory, J. J. *The Vanity Fair Gallery – A Collector's Guide to the Caricatures*. A. S. Barnes (USA), 1979.
Swanton, E. W. (editor). *The Barclays World of Cricket*. Collins, 1980.
Swanton, E. W. *A History of Cricket*. Allen and Unwin, 1962.
Tayler, A. Chevallier. *The Empire's Cricketers*. Fine Art Society, 1905.
Tomlins, R. *Classic Cricket Cards*. Constable, 1980.
Tomlins, R. *More Classic Cricket Cards*. Constable, 1981.
Warner, P. F. *Lord's*. Harrap, 1946.
Wisden Cricketers' Almanack 1966.

PLACES TO VISIT

The main collection in England is the Cricket Memorial Gallery at Lord's Cricket Ground, London NW8. This is open on match days, Mondays to Saturdays, from 10.30 a.m. until 5 p.m. It may be visited on other occasions, as can the MCC Library, by prior application to the Curator.

Readers in North America should visit the C. Christopher Morris Cricket Library and Collection at Haverford College, Pennsylvania, 19041. There is also the fine Auty Library at Ridley College, St Catherine's, Ontario.

Australia is well served by the museums at the Sydney and Melbourne Cricket Grounds. The latter has a particularly fine display of ceramics from the noted collection of Mr Anthony Baer.

Trap-ball is a very old game and is similar to cricket in some respects, but not its ancestor. It is still played in parts of south-east England. The trap shown here probably dates from the late seventeenth century.

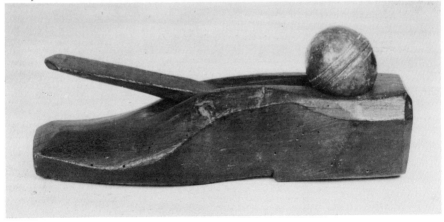